NATURE DETECTIVE

Coarse Fishing

A Photographic Guide

Martin Ford

WAYLAND

Acknowledgements:
Alamy 2BL, 32-33 Buiten-Beeld; Martin Ford
02BR, 12, 13B; FLPA/ Jack Perks 16-17T; 30
Yannick Gouguenhei; Shutterstock.com 1, 8,
8B aleksandr hunta; 3TL, 6T, 36, 46 Kletr; 3TR,
14B thd_fon; 04B Erni; 05T Jon Bilous; 6C
Dmitry Eagle Orlov; 6B Kushch Dmitry; 7T David
Guyler; 7B CrackerClips Stock Media; 9 Mike
Pellinni; 10 Leene; 11 James Ding; 11 Yuryev
Pavel; 13T Pascal Ylia; 14-15 Krasowit; 15T,
17T Kovalchuk Oleksandr; 15C piotr.ma; 15B
Erni; 16, 31 Rudmer Zwerver; 17B Jane Rix; 18T
schankz; 18B Everything; 19BL Imageman; 19BR
morisfoto; 19C Lonely Walker; 19T Constantine
Pankin; 21 Vladimir Wrangel; 22-23 iliuta goean;
24TL, 24-25 jack perks; 20-21, 24-25, 26-27
(backgrounds), 38-39 Morozov Maxim; 26-27
Aliexxandar; 28 Emilio 100; 29 Geza Farkas;
34, 42-43 Vladimir Wrangel; 34-35 Martin
Pelanek; 39 Kletr; 41 Krzysztof Odziomek; 42
Kuttelvaserova Stuchelova; 44 MilanMarkovic78;
44 CkyBe; 44-45 Krzysztof Odziomek; 46-47
Martin Pelanek; 48-49 Halfpoint; 48 HTU; 50-51
Halfpoint; 50 godrick; 51, 56 Bildagentur Zoonar
GmbH; 52 Dennis Jacobsen; 53 Gallinago_
media; 54-55 Zurbanov Alexei; 54 belizar; 55
Preobrajenskiy; 56 alslutsky; 57 Czesznak;
Wikimedia Commons/Karelj 26; 58/59 Wayland
Archives

Contents

What is coarse fishing?

Coarse fishing is one of three different kinds of angling. It covers catching freshwater species that are non-migratory, including eels, but excluding trout and salmon. Trout and salmon fall into the 'game fishing' category, while species that live in the sea come under the 'salt water fishing' or 'sea fishing' category.

Let's go fishing!

To be good at coarse fishing you will need to be quiet, observant, extremely patient and, above all, respectful to nature! Coarse fishing can take place on small farm ponds, lakes, canals and some rivers. Each venue will be home to a variety of coarse fishing species, offering great opportunities to practise your fishing skills.

Coarse fishing habitats

Most new anglers will start with a visit to a small farm pond, where they can catch smaller species of fish such as rudd, roach, perch and gudgeon. Others will try their luck on a local club lake, much bigger in size and holding bigger species such as tench, bream and carp. A few will venture onto the canal systems, where many different species can be found. And some will choose to fish the river systems, tackling running water and species such as dace, chub and barbel.

Wherever you choose to pursue your angling, it is important to stick to the basic rules of coarse fishing: be courteous to other anglers and take care of the environment you are in; don't leave any litter or discarded fishing line, as this may cause serious damage to wildlife.

Coarse fishing safety

Fishing is great fun, and exploring your area to find places to fish can be as much of an adventure as angling itself. But you also need to take great care to make sure you don't hurt yourself or go against local rules and laws when you're out and about.

Be on the lookout

When looking for a suitable place to fish, be aware of the dangers you may encounter. On canal systems, there are many areas that have overhead pylons carrying live electrical currents. If accidentally touched by a carbon pole or fishing rod, they can cause severe burns and serious accidents. Look up before you fish and be aware of your surroundings.

Rivers can be dangerous when in flood, especially in winter. A non-swimmer may struggle to get out of the flowing water should they fall in. Avoid accidents by sitting back from the edge of the river bank. Fish with an adult until you are confident in your own abilities.

If you are setting off without an adult, tell someone where you are going. Make sure your mobile phone is fully charged, carry a first aid kit for cuts and grazes and take hand sanitizer – water may carry diseases, so it's important to keep your hands clean.

Coarse fishing law

If you are under 12 and live in the UK, you don't need to have a rod licence to fish for coarse fishing species. However, you may still be required to pay for a day or season ticket to fish at your chosen water. A good source of information on licences and individual club permits is a local tackle shop.

Once you reach the age of 12, you will need to purchase a national rod licence. This is available from the Environment Agency and most UK post offices, as well as online at www.gov.uk/fishing-licences. If you fail to produce a rod licence to a patrolling Environment Agency officer, you may need to appear in court and pay a heavy fine.

If you are planning on fishing abroad, make sure you find out local laws and rules.

Where to go

There are many different venues that are open to the coarse angler, some wild and some man-made. Here are just a few to choose from!

Commercial fishery

When visiting a commercial fishery, you will often find small, but well-stocked waters. Catching lots of fish can be achieved quickly, because of the high stock densities. As a beginner, you can gain a lot of confidence and also learn quickly when fishing this type of water. Commercial fishery is also the type of venue where most competitions take place. Fisheries tend to work on a day-ticket basis, where you pay before you start to fish.

Stream

There are always plenty of coarse fish species sheltering in small brooks and streams. There are likely to be roach, usually in good numbers. As most streams are shallow, the deeper parts of the water course are likely to hold more fish, so are worth looking for. However, you should check before fishing, as streams that contain game fish may be controlled by a private game fishing club. In this case, coarse anglers will not be allowed to fish.

River

Most main river systems hold a large amount of coarse fishing species, in particular bream, chub and barbel. Once again, you will need to check that you able to fish before doing so. Most river systems are usually controlled by angling clubs and may offer a day or season ticket. Unlike most other types of fishery, rivers can be dangerous, as they flood after heavy rain. It is important to take care, especially when standing on river banks – they are often eroded by floods.

Please remember that all river systems have a closed season; fishing (for fish other than trout and salmon) is forbidden from 15th March to 15th June.

Farm pond

Small farm ponds are mostly privately owned; they are open to the public and will allow you to fish for a very cheap day ticket price. They don't tend to be as well stocked as some of the commercial fisheries, but will often hold bigger fish. The farm pond will hold species such as tench, carp, perch and roach. It's worth doing some research on the internet for farm land in your area, and checking on maps to see if any of them offer water. Some farmers will even let you fish for free, provided you have asked first.

Don't forget: To fish any of types of venue you must first ensure that, if you are 12 years or older, you are in possession of a rod licence.

Stillwater

Natural stillwater can be anything from a small public lake to one of 100 acres or more. They are all worth investigating. Some will be private, others run by angling clubs. As always, you will need to research your venues before fishing there. Natural stillwaters may have received stocks of fish, or may be neglected, so if you are keen to catch lots of fish, like at a commercial fishery, you'll have to investigate further. Club-controlled stillwaters usually offer good fishing and will have stocks of most coarse species. Bream, tench, roach, rudd, carp, perch and even eels often live in this type of environment.

Canal

Most canals hold many different species of coarse fish. Canal basins, where canal barges moor, are always good holding points for shoal fish such as bream. Marinas are also ideal, but check that you are allowed to fish before starting to do so, as many marinas don't grant access to anglers. However, a lot of the UK canal network is leased to angling clubs, so there is bound to be a local club stretch somewhere near you.

Fishing tackle

The essential items for catching fish are rods, reels, lines, floats, hooks and weights. There are different approaches that are used to catch fish; most commonly, these are float fishing with a rod and reel or whip, and leger fishing with a leger rod and reel.

Float fishing rod

Float rods tend to be 3–4 m long. For smaller species, such as roach, float rods tend to be quite flexible in the tip; they are slightly stiffer when used for commercial fishery carp angling. There are usually three sections of rod which join together: a tip, a middle and a butt section. Match this type of rod with a lightweight, fixed spool reel, capable of holding 100 m of fine line.

Whip fishing

Many beginners start off with a whip, a 2–4 m length of carbon or fibreglass. The line is tied directly to the end of the whip. You then flick the whip forwards, propelling the float and baited hook into the water. Wait for a bite, lift the whip and swing the fish to your hand! Whips are only suitable for smaller species, weighing between 30 and 220 grams.

Leger fishing

Legering is fishing on the bottom of the water with a weight, using a rod designed for leger fishing. It is called a quivertip rod, as the tip of the rod is ultra-fine; it is also often brightly coloured. The angler casts out, sinks the line down and sets the tip of the rod just above the water in a rod rest. When a fish bites, the soft tip starts to 'quiver' and is slowly tugged, which indicates that a fish has been hooked.

Reel

The reel you use will depend on the type of rod you are matching it with, and the species you intend to catch. Fixed spool reels are most common and come in many sizes. Some specialist anglers prefer a 'centrepin reel', which has a free revolving movement, allowing the tow of a river to pull line as the float moves downstream.

Net

You will need a landing net to land your catch safely. Make sure your net is suited to the species you are fishing for and that it uses a soft mesh material; this is kinder to fish. Some anglers use a keepnet. This is a long (2–4 m) tube of netting. Fish are carefully placed in during a session, then weighed and released at the end.

Line

There are thousands of different items of tackle that a budding coarse angler is likely to encounter, but one of the essentials is definitely the line. It should suit the species of fish you want to catch: small fish – fine lines, big fish – strong lines. Seek advice from your local tackle shop or an expert at a fishery to help you make your choice.

Floats

Floats come in different sizes, shapes and colours. There are floats for stillwater (wagglers) and floats for running waters (stick floats). Stillwater floats are generally thin in profile, while river floats tend to be bulkier, with more buoyancy for running water fishing. Pole floats are a little more specialised. They are selected for the type of fish and also for the type of bait you are going to use. Once again, it is best to ask for advice from the professionals!

Weights and split shot

Split shot are small weights with a 'split'. They are pinched onto the line in order to weigh down a float. The aim is to have the minimum amount of the tip showing, as this offers less resistance when the fish picks up the bait. Legering weights are larger and have a swivel fixed into the body. They can be clipped onto a specialist lead clip when fishing for bigger species, such as carp.

Hooks

The general rule for hooks is, small fish – small hook, big fish – big hook! It's important to match the size of the bait to the hook, so for example a single maggot would suit a size 20 hook, whereas a cube of luncheon meat would be better suited to a size 6 hook. Hooks come as barbed or barbless, but most fisheries will state that barbless hooks must be used – a barbless hook can be easily removed.

And finally...

There is one tool that every coarse angler should carry: a disgorger. It's used to remove hooks that have caught further back in the fish's mouth. Don't go fishing without one!

Baits

Every coarse angler will have a favourite bait that they prefer to use, maybe because it has caught them a lot of fish. There are lots of different baits – some specialist and others that are more easily available, even from

Maggots

The humble maggot has been at the forefront of coarse fishing for generations. It is probably the most widely used bait by far. Maggots are specially bred in large fly houses and can be bought by the pint from a reliable tackle shop. Make sure you have a container with a sealable lid when collecting your maggots from the shop. It must also have small air holes in the lid so that the maggots can breathe.

If maggots are kept extremely cold, in the fridge at home (they will not contaminate domestic food), they will stop the natural process of turning into flies. Beware – the warmer they get, the quicker the process will speed up. If they escape in your home, you will eventually have flies hatching out everywhere for days!

Bait tip: Maggots can be used as a single bait, as double baits hooked back-to-back, or indeed in bunches on big hooks for big fish!

Casters

A caster is a maggot at the stage when it becomes a chrysalis and starts to turn into a fly. Casters are small, maggot-sized brown shells. Lighter ones will sink, darker ones will float. They are a great bait for roach and rudd and can be purchased from tackle shops. They will need to be used on the day of purchase or the day after, before they turn into flies! Casters and hempseed are a great bait combination, as hemp sinks very fast, along with light casters, while the dark casters sink slowly or float. This keeps fish searching the water for food.

Bait tip: Bury the small hook right inside the caster shell when fishing for species such as roach.

Hempseed

Hempseed is very cheap but effective as a bait. It can be used in conjunction with other baits such as casters and maggots. It is a seed, as the name suggests, and is sold in its dried form. You will need to soak it in cold water for 24 hours, before bringing it to the boil and then leaving to cool. Once boiled, the hemp seed splits to reveal a small white 'ear', and it's this that the fish find attractive!

Bait tip: Hemp can be used as a feedbait when fishing using a hookbait called a tare – another form of seed, but bigger than hemp.

Worms

Lobworms and small redworms are both effective baits and catch a variety of species from carp to bream. Worms can be bought in small tubs or indeed kilo bags from the tackle shop… or they can be dug from the garden! Worms can be fished whole or in chopped sections, depending on the size and species of fish you are after. Push the hook through the raised part of the worm, called the saddle. It is the toughest part of the worm's body.

Bait tip: If you are using a whole worm, attach a small section of rubber band once you have hooked the worm. This will stop it from wriggling around and escaping from the hook!

Sweetcorn

Everyday sweetcorn, available from supermarkets, is a great coarse fishing bait. Tench, carp and bream love it! Sweetcorn can be used straight from the tin. One or more grains can be fished, depending on the species you are fishing and size of hook you are using. Sweetcorn is quite tough and a small hook can be buried inside a single grain when fishing for shy species such as rudd.

Bait tip: Try mixing two grains of corn with two or three maggots when fishing for summer tench.

Bread

There are many ways to use bread as coarse bait. A few slices put through a liquidiser will give you groundbait that will sink very slowly, clouding the water and attracting fish in to feed. Or simply pinch a bit of bread from a slice and mould it around a hook– perfect for big roach!

Bait tip: Bread flakes and maggots mixed together are a super hookbait for tench and big roach.

Tinned meats

Tinned meats such as spam have caught many specimen fish over the years. It can be cut into small cubes and mounted on a big hook for species such as barbel and larger carp, or finely chopped and mixed in groundbait for small carp and bream.

Bait tip: Try flavouring your meat hookbaits with curry powder or paprika – barbel love it!

groundbait

pellets

Barbel

Scientific name: *Barbus barbus*
Size: Average 1.4 kg
Fact: The current British rod caught record stands at 9.553 kg
Habitat: Freshwater rivers and commercial stillwater fisheries
Natural Food: Invertebrates, small fish,

Best baits:
Barbel can be caught on maggots, casters, sweetcorn, meat baits, cheese paste, pellets and specialist carp baits such as boilies.

The barbel is a very powerful fish and kilogram-for-kilogram is regarded by many as the hardest fish to catch from a river! It's designed for scavenging the bottom of a fast-flowing river. It has an underslung mouth and is equipped with two pairs of barbs on either side of its head which are used to detect food items in the gravel of the river bed.

Young barbel tend to move and feed together in small shoals. Bigger barbel are loners, preferring their own company. They will often become territorial, frequenting just a small section of river where food is easy to come by. The barbel is a long, sleek specimen, built for speed and power, and perfectly equipped for the fast flow of a river. The body is golden brown in colour.

It is always advisable with river-caught barbel, particularly big ones, to support them in the water after capture until they have regained their strength and are able to swim off back into the current.

Best method: Legering on rivers with a swim feeder

Bream

Scientific name: *Abramis brama*

Size: Average 1 kg

Fact: The current British rod caught record stands at 10.291 kg

Habitat: Freshwater ponds, lakes, canals and slow moving rivers

Natural food: Crustaceans, fish eggs, leeches, midge larvae

Best baits:
Bream love worms, casters, sweetcorn, bread flake, pellets and high protein carp fishing baits such as boilies.

There are two species of freshwater bream: the silver bream and the bronze bream. It's the bronze bream that the coarse angler is most likely to encounter, as the silver bream is not that widespread and is a lot smaller in size. The bronze bream travels in vast shoals; they can be likened to a herd of grazing cows, as they spend hours grazing over areas in search of food items!

The colour of the bronze bream will vary depending on its age. Young bream are a creamy pale silver, while the older fish tend to be of a creamy underside, bronze flanks and a dark brown back. Bream are a deep bodied, almost flat-sided species that spend much of their time patrolling the bottom of lakes and slow-moving rivers in search of food.

Once you have located bream it is likely that you will catch more than one, as they are a shoal fish. They will expel small bubbles when feeding ravenously on the bottom, and will often cause the water to cloud up as they root around looking for food items in the silt.

There are many different types of carp, but the mirror carp, common carp, leather carp and the crucian carp are the most common. The coarse angler is likely to encounter the mirror and common carp which can grow to very big sizes! The common carp is covered in scales, while the mirror carp is partially scaled and the leather carp has no scales at all!

The colour of the body may vary, depending on habitat. Carp living in clear water will often have black backs, but most carp are generally a golden-brown colour with a darker back. Carp can be caught from a variety of different waters, but big specimens are found in specialist fishing lakes that only stock carp of a larger size.

Carp spend hours sifting through the bottom debris in search of foods and are armed with pharyngeal teeth at the back of the mouth, which are capable of crushing even the hardest of snail and mussel shells! Carp have a great sense of smell and can home in on artificial baits, especially fish-meal flavoured ones! They are able to see extremely well and have more sensitive eyesight than most humans. However, they do have a blind spot right in front of, and directly below, their mouth, due to side-mounted eyes.

Like all fish, carp are cold blooded creatures. Therefore, trying to catch a carp in the depths of winter can sometimes be a struggle! Warmer water temperatures speed up their metabolism while colder water temperatures will slow metabolism and digestion.

Best method: legering

Mirror carp

Scientific name: *Cyprinus carpio*

Size: Average 2 kg

Fact: The current British rod caught record stands at 30.875 kg

Habitat: Freshwater ponds, lakes, canals and slow-moving rivers

Natural food: Crustaceans, water fleas, freshwater shrimp, molluscs, bloodworm

Best baits:
Carp are generally caught on high-protein specialist carp baits such as boilies. Bread, maggots, worms and sweetcorn will also work.

Chub

Scientific name: *Leuciscus cephalus*

Size: Average 2 kg

Fact: The current British rod caught record stands at 4.224 kg

Habitat: Freshwater ponds, lakes, canals and rivers

Natural food: Invertebrates, small fish, insects, berries, fruit, crayfish

Best baits:
Chub can be caught on maggots, casters, meat baits, worms, slugs, cheese paste, pellets, sweetcorn, bread and even high protein carp baits such as boilies.

boilies

Chub are traditionally a river or flowing water species. Now, however, they are widespread throughout canals and even stillwater gravel pits, which tend to offer anglers the best chance of catching a record-sized specimen!

Chub are predatory. They live together in shoals as young fish, but tend to become loners as they get larger. On rivers, chub can often be found in the slower-moving water, under trailing tree branches, waiting for the next item of food to be swept downstream by the current. In shallow river systems, it's possible to observe chub sifting through the gravel beds, hunting for all manner of food items that are disturbed, such as small crayfish and caddis larvae.

The chub has a long, streamlined body covered in greyish-black scales. Its back is brown with a slight green-golden tinge, and its belly is a vibrant white. They have a very large mouth and have pharyngeal teeth at the back of the throat. They use these teeth for crushing food such as whole slugs, small minnow or an armour-plated crayfish!

27

Crucian carp

Scientific name: *Carassius carassius*
Size: Average 0.5 kg
Fact: The current British rod caught record stands at 2.098 kg
Habitat: Lakes and ponds
Natural food: Insects, snails, leeches, bloodworm

Best baits:
Maggots, pellets, sweetcorn and bread flakes.

The crucian carp is the smallest type of carp, and a crucian of 1 kg is considered a specimen fish. True crucian carp are hard to find and only a few waters contain genuine crucians, as interbreeding has led to a rise in hybrid strains. They are short and dumpy in appearance and have a rich golden colour to their flanks. Younger crucians can be a dull silver in colour.

The fins on a true crucian carp are rounded, as is the main dorsal fin, which is convex, unlike other carp who have concave (rounded inwards) dorsal fins. A further identification factor is that the crucian has no barbules, unlike a standard carp, and the lower fins can be a slight orange colour.

Crucian carp are very shy when it comes to angler's bait, often giving false bites as they play around with the bait. The crucian tends to spend a lot of time in hiding and is more confident in feeding at dawn and dusk. Bigger crucians will travel in small shoals of a dozen or so as they hunt through the bottom silt in search of a meal.

Best method: Float fishing with a small crystal waggler

The dace is often referred to as the silver dart, as it 'darts' around investigating all manner of possible food items. Once located, they are fairly easy to catch, as they congregate together in large shoals, searching through the upper, middle and lower layers of the water for food.

The species has a very slender body, yellow eyes and they are a bluey-grey colour with silvery flanks. The tail has a deep fork and is built for speed and for reacting to the flow of the river current. Although primarily a flowing water species, dace are also present in many canal systems.

Dace are often confused with the chub, another river species. The difference between the two is in the anal and dorsal fins – the dace's are both concave. Their feeding habits can give their location away, as, like the rudd, they will swirl at insects on the surface and spend much of their time feeding in the upper layers.

Best method: Float fishing with a stick float on flowing water

Dace

Scientific name: *Cleuciscus leuciscus*

Size: Average 0.2 kg

Fact: The current British rod caught record stands at 0.599 kg

Habitat: Freshwater rivers, streams and canals

Natural food: Worms, algae, insects, snails, crustaceans

Best baits: Dace can be caught on maggots, casters, worms and bread.

Eel

Scientific name: *Anguilla anguilla*

Size: Average 0.5 kg

Fact: The current British rod caught record stands at 5.046 kg

Habitat: Freshwater rivers, lakes, ponds streams and canals

Natural food: Insect larvae, fish fry

Best baits: Small pieces of dead bait roach (cut with scissors), lob worms, maggots and casters.

The eel is often looked upon as a menace to some coarse anglers. This is because it can writhe and wriggle and tangle up fishing line in no time, covering everything in slime as it does so! For a few specialist anglers, big eels have become a way of life and that's the only species that they fish for!

Eels can be abundant in canal systems and even in ponds and rivers. But the bigger eels, over 1.5 kg, are sought after on deep, neglected waters where they have become trapped over time and grown on to become worthy targets.

Eels are fish eaters, so will readily take fish as bait. They are always caught on the bottom. Eels are long and lean in appearance with slimy bodies. They have a large mouth that has a protruding lower jaw containing huge amounts of tiny teeth! The dorsal and anal fins form a continuous line around the tail, allowing the eel to move extremely fast, both backwards and forwards! The eel's colouring changes with maturity; generally, it is black or brown with yellow or silver sides and a white belly.

Gudgeon

Scientific name: *Gobio gobio*
Size: Average 0.03 kg
Fact: The current British rod caught record stands at 0.141 kg
Habitat: Lakes, rivers, and canals
Natural food: Invertebrates, midge, caddis fly larvae

Best baits:
Maggots

Gudgeon are bottom feeders, scavenging what they can from the silt and mud. They are widespread throughout canal systems, lakes and even slow moving rivers. They are often mistaken for baby barbel; however, the gudgeon has only two barbules either side of its mouth, whereas the barbel has four. Gudgeon rarely grow much bigger than 15 cm in length. They have a round, slightly elongated body with quite a large head and a very flat belly.

The gudgeon is dull in colour to help it blend in with its habitat and to protect it from predators, namely the perch! It is a muted silvery blue with pale yellow flanks which sport dark spots.

The gudgeon is a shoal fish and is probably amongst the easiest of species to catch on rod and line. If you catch one, you'll catch another very shortly. They are a very good species to target for the coarse fishing beginner. The more experienced competition angler can amass big weights during a match, weighing in 500 or more gudgeon!

35

Perch

Scientific name: *Perca fluviatilis*

Size: Average 0.2 kg

Fact: The current British rod caught record stands at 2.806 kg

Habitat: Freshwater ponds, lakes, canals and slow moving rivers

Natural food: Planktonic organisms, invertebrates, small fry (including its own type)

Best baits:
Worms, maggots or small dead baits such as minnows and roach.

For many coarse anglers, the perch is a fish that will always bring fond memories, as in many cases it's the first fish that was caught! Perch are relatively easy to catch. This is because their instinct dictates that they spend a lot of time close to the banks of ponds and lakes, searching out any food that might come their way. The perch is a very colourful fish with a green-brown back and a series of strikingly dark vertical bars across its sides, tipped with bright red-orange under its fins!

For the beginner, a word of warning when handling a perch: they have a very spikey dorsal fin which, although not venomous, can give a nasty prick. The perch also has flattened spikes on each side of the gill plate and has very rough skin – all for protection against other predators! Small perch can be caught one after another as they travel in shoals; bigger perch, over 1 kg, are solitary creatures and require a more specialist approach of someone who is very skilled at catching perch.

Best method: Float fishing with a crystal waggler or legering with a straight bomb

The pike is feared by many, yet a lot of coarse anglers go on to specialise in pike fishing, probably because pike can grow to such big sizes. Young pike have flecked yellow stripes on a green body. As they mature, the yellow fades to reveal light spots on an olive-green background and a pale underside. The fins are a red-to-orange colour, speckled with black spots.

The pike is built for ambush tactics and its colouring allows it to blend into the underwater vegetation extremely well, as it sits in wait for its prey to pass by. The pike's mouth is loaded with razor-sharp teeth, allowing a firm grip on its prey.

Once caught, it requires a lot of skill to remove the hook from a large pike. If you are considering fishing for pike, you should ensure that you carry a pair of

Best method: Float fishing, legering and spinning

Best baits: Pike are usually caught using dead baits such as trout, smelt, roach or mackerel.

Pike

Scientific name: *Esox lucius*

Size: Average 1 kg

Fact: The current British rod caught record stands at 21.234 kg

Habitat: Lakes, ponds, rivers and canals

Natural food: Invertebrates, daphnia, small live fish

long-nosed pliers, or forceps, wire cutters, a large landing net and an unhooking mat to lay your fish on. Barbless treble hooks are highly recommended for pike fishing, as they can be removed very easily. You should allow the pike time to recover in your large landing net before you release it back into the water – they often take a while to recover from a capture.

Roach are a shoal fish, and will gather in their hundreds. There is great safety in numbers, particularly when you are small in size, silver in colour and are the main prey for species such as pike and zander.

Roach can be identified by their bright crimson-red tail and dorsal fin. However, they are not to be confused with rudd, a similar-sized species with almost identical colouration. The difference can be seen in the mouth, which protrudes downwards, while the rudd's mouth curves upward for surface feeding.

Most fisheries contain large quantities of small roach, as they are prolific breeders. Most will be in the 0.2–0.3 kg-bracket. Occasionally, on bigger waters; coarse anglers may encounter a specimen upwards of 1 kg, which is a fish of a lifetime for this species!

On fast-flowing rivers, roach populations will often move away from the main current. They can be found in big numbers in back streams off the main river flow.

Best method: Float fishing with a fine-tipped waggler float

Roach

Scientific name: *Rutilus rutilus*

Size: Average 0.05 kg

Fact: The current British rod caught record stands at 1.927 kg

Habitat: Freshwater ponds, lakes, canals and slow-moving rivers

Natural food: Freshwater shrimp, insects, small molluscs, midge larvae

Best baits:
Roach can be caught on a variety of baits, such as maggots, casters, worms and bread.

Rudd

Scientific name: Scardinius erythrophthalmus
Size: Average 0.15 kg
Fact: The current British rod caught record
stands at 2.097 kg
Habitat: Freshwater ponds, lakes and canals
Natural food: Freshwater shrimps, insects,
midge larvae

Best baits:
Rudd can be caught on a variety of baits such as maggots, casters, corn and particularly bread flake for specimen-sized rudd.

Rudd are often classed as the ghost of angling and big rudd in particular can be very, very shy! Patience and stealth are a requirement when seeking specimen-sized rudd. Like the roach, smaller rudd move in shoals, so if you catch one, others will be present. Bigger specimens are more likely to travel together in groups of a dozen or so and can disappear as quickly as they have arrived!

Feeding in the upper layers of the water, rudd often take small emerging insects as they rise from the bottom as well as swirling to take flies from the surface on a warm summer day.

A rudd over 1 kg is classed as a specimen. They can be identified by their almost greenish-golden flanks and bright red fins. Rudd have a slightly upward-curved mouth with a protruding bottom jaw for taking food items off the surface; they also have noticeably large eyes for good sight!

Rudd like to spend time near cover such as reedmace, and lily pads, as not only does the cover provide safety, but also food. They will give their location away by swirling on the surface as they sip at insects!

Tench

Scientific name: *Tinca tinca*

Size: Average 1 kg

Fact: The current British rod caught record stands at 6.899 kg

Habitat: Freshwater ponds, lakes, canals and slow-moving rivers

Natural food: Bloodworms, crustaceans, daphnia

Best baits: Tench love maggots, casters, sweetcorn, bread flakes and lob worms.

There are two main types of tench. The most common, and the one the coarse angler is likely to encounter, is the green tench, which is very distinguishable by its olive green colouration and tiny vibrant red eyes. It's often referred to as 'the doctor fish', because folklore has it that the slime or mucus that covers its body has special healing powers.

The other type of tench is the golden tench. It is gold in colour and often sold in garden centres as a garden pond fish, due to fact that it is much smaller in size.

Big tench are powerful and have large tail fins to propel them away from danger. Female tench are usually bigger than males. Tench are associated with early morning and late evening fishing. They will often give their location away, as they expel tiny bubbles that rise to the surface while they root and grub about the bottom in search of food.

Best method: Float fishing

Zander

Scientific name: Sander lucioperca
Size: Average 1.5 kg
Fact: The current British rod caught record stands at 9.667
Habitat: Freshwater ponds, lakes, canals and slow moving rivers
Natural food: Live fry

Best baits:
Dead baits cut into half sections, worms, spinners and jelly lures

The zander is very closely related to the perch, has a similar shape to a pike and carries the spines on the dorsal fin that the perch also has. It is often referred to as a pike or perch, however, the zander is not a hybrid of the pike and perch, as is often believed. The zander was introduced illegally into British waters, on the Anglian Broads in the mid 20th century. It has thrived and become widespread throughout rivers, canals and stillwaters.

The zander is a grey-green colour with pale dark bars running down the flank, melting away into a cream-white belly. The mouth houses an array of tiny needle-sharp teeth and its eyes are jet black.

This cunning predator has the ability to hunt and see in the deepest, murkiest water. It has been caught at depths of 5.5 m! Bigger zander prefer to lay-up in the deep water during the day, and to hunt their prey at night, under the cover of darkness. On river systems, the zander's preferred meal is another coarse fish – the bleak. The zander will often give its presence away by striking near the surface as it closes in for the kill!

47

Kingfisher

Scientific name: *Alcedo atthis*
Natural food: Small fish and aquatic insects
Where to see: Still water lakes, ponds, canals, slow-moving rivers and streams

There is no angler more skilled than the Kingfisher – hence its name! Although a small bird, it is incredibly fast as it flits between bankside perches, on the hunt for small fish and aquatic insects to feed itself and its young. It has razor-sharp eyesight and can spot a small fish from a high perch above the water, waiting patiently for an opportunity to dive down and snatch it.

If you sit quietly and your fishing rod is set in a rest out in front of you, overhanging the water, there's every chance that, out of the blue, a kingfisher will land on the tip of your rod, making it bounce and sway momentarily as it lands! Your rod tip is simply seen as a great vantage point above the water's edge that the kingfisher can plunge downwards from, into the water below to snatch some unwary fry from its depths.

The kingfisher is unmistakable, with its plumage of vibrant blues, greens and oranges. Although most sightings take place during the warmer months of summer, kingfishers can be seen at any time of year.

Heron

Scientific name: *Alcedo atthis*
Natural food: Small fish and
  aquatic insects
Where to see: Still water lakes, ponds,
  canals, slow-moving rivers and streams

The gracious, very sleek grey heron is an out-and-out master at catching fish, and even small mammals such as voles. The heron can often be spotted quietly wading along the margins, stopping dead in its tracks as it peers down into the shallow water below, ready to plunge its head beneath the surface to grab an unsuspecting meal.

The heron is a very shy creature and will often fly off if disturbed. You have a better chance of seeing one if you are already sitting and quietly fishing, and one comes into land near to you. Don't move, and you'll be able to observe.

The heron stands up to 1 m tall and has extremely long brown legs, enabling it to wade in shallow water with ease. Herons also have a very long, spear-like beak which is a pinkish-yellow in colour and perfectly shaped for catching fish and other aquatic creatures. The body of the heron is grey with a grey-white underside and its neck and head feature a distinct black stripe extending from the eye to the black crest. It is a very patient hunter and will stand still for long periods of time, just waiting for the right opportunity to pounce.

Sand martin

Scientific name: *Riparia riparia*
Natural food: Insects
Where to see: Stillwaters, river banks

As the name suggests, the sand martin nests in sandy landscapes, in cliff walls, river banks and even old quarry ponds and lakes. It will dig into the side of a sand wall, making a burrow, and will return year after year if its chosen nesting site remains safe.

The tiny sand martin is brown on the back and pale white below the belly. It has a black beak and small brown legs. Sand martins are often mistaken for swallows, due to their similar size. However, in comparison to the swallow, the sand martin has a quick, jerky, un-smooth action to its flight.

Sand martins are summer visitors to UK shores and are often the first to return from South Africa where they have spent the winter months. They can be seen in the UK as early as March. Their main diet is spiders and insects, and they look for them late in the day, flitting over the surface of still waters, feasting on all manner of water insects.

Swallow

Scientific name: *Hirundo rustica*
Natural food: Insects
Where to see: Large lakes, ponds

The swallow is a bird that the coarse angler is likely to encounter, especially when fishing on larger lakes and gravel pits. Throughout May to October swallows will often gather at a large expanse of water, late in the evening, and can be observed swooping and diving, skimming the water and acrobatically picking off insects from the surface.

Swallows can be identified by their blue glossy backs, pale underside and distinct red throat feathers. Their tails are long, like a streamer, and are built for precision flying. They are exceptionally agile, as one mistake may mean a missed meal! In large numbers, they can cause quite a stir as they swoop and dive across the surface of a lake, taking insects as they go.

Swallows communicate to alert one another of danger or food sources, resulting in many different calls and songs. They are a joy to watch and often mark the beginning of spring with their arrival, staying throughout the warmer months before flying south for the winter in October.

Bat

Scientific name: *Chiroptera*
Natural food: Insects
Where to see: Large lakes that have surrounding woodlands

Bats can be seen close to large expanses of freshwater late in the evening and at dawn. This is because they feed on all manner of hatching insects that can usually be found amongst the bankside vegetation. Sometimes they will skim the water with incredible precision, picking off large mayflies mid-flight.

Bats are nocturnal, which means that they are mostly awake at night, and asleep during the day. They need to find their prey, and successfully catch it, in very low light. They achieve this with the help of a technique called echolocation, which involves sending out signals and interpreting the returning echoes to locate prey. Bats can also use their eyes to see, but echolocation is far more precise when it is dark.

When fishing in the evening, you will often have bats flitting around your head and fishing equipment in the darkness; but notice that they never crash into objects – they are the masters of night flight!

Frog

Scientific name: *Anura*
Natural food: Small invertebrates
Where to see: Still waters, ponds, canals

The coarse angler is very likely to come across either the frog or its offspring, the tadpole. You can't mistake what a frog looks like – brown or green, with long back legs and webbed toes. Its large eyes, perched on either side of the upper part of the head, have an almost 360-degree window of sight, which means the frog can see almost everything around it without moving its head! Frogs can often be heard before they are seen, as they communicate with each other by croaking loudly.

Typically found around ponds, canals, rivers and lakes, the frog needs to be near water in order to survive. It also lays its spawn in the water, generating thousands of tiny tadpoles. Both adult frogs and their offspring are an important food source for other animals, such as snakes and even freshwater fish including pike.

Frogs mostly eat insects, snails, frogs and worms, which they catch with their incredibly sticky, long tongue! They don't use teeth to chew their prey; instead, they swallow everything whole. The frog has many glands around the body and particularly near the head. These exude toxic substances, which in turn help to keep its skin moist in very warm weather.

Dragonfly

Scientific name: *Odonata*
Natural food: Insects
Where to see: Stillwaters, ponds, canals, rivers

The coarse angler cannot fail to see the brightly coloured dragonflies as they fly around the plants and reeds that surround most waters. They are easily confused with the Damsel fly, a much smaller species.

The dragonfly is a ruthless predator, not just as an adult, but also in the early stages of life as aquatic larvae. Many years of its life are spent under water as a nymph, before emerging to the surface and hatching. During the underwater period it is capable of preying on very small fry and indeed this forms a staple part of the diet, which enables it to grow and emerge to the surface to hatch.

When newly hatched, adult dragonflies will crawl from their casing and spread their wings to dry out before they can fly. The coarse angler who is keen with a camera will be able to get some great close-up shots.

Grass snake

Scientific name: *Natrix natrix*
Natural food: Frogs, tadpoles, toads, small fish, mice
Where to see: Stillwaters, ponds, slow-moving rivers

Grass snakes love to be near water as it provides plenty of food, with tadpoles, frogs, toads and even small mice being on the menu.

Old quarry ponds that have banksides built up from sandstone and bricks that have been covered in soil provide the ideal home for the grass snake to thrive in, as it can slip away to a honeycomb of holes and tunnels, getting deep underground to safety. To stand the best chance of seeing a grass snake in its natural environment will require a stealthy approach, as they are reactive to vibration and noise. If you come across one sunbathing on a pathway or grass verge near to the water, keep still, don't move and just observe!

The grass snake can grow up to 1.5 m in length, but on average is around 1 m. It's easy to identify by the black, yellow and white crescent-shaped collar marking on the neck. The body is olive green to dark green with distinct black bars. Grass snakes do not have a venomous bite, but can put on a very aggressive display if disturbed. If handled, they can discharge a very smelly liquid, which is best avoided!

Half blood knot

You can use the half blood knot to secure your hook, ready to catch even the largest of coarse fish!

1 Thread the line through the eye and double up above it.

2 Twist the hook around eight times. Keep the twists tight and grab the loose end.

3 Push the hook through the lowest loop between the top of the eye and the first twist.

4 Push the loose end through the loop you have made. This is called the 'truck'.

5 Wet the knot with a little spit and start to tighten it. Pull the knot down to the eye.

6 Hold the knot tight for three seconds, then trim it off.

Figure of eight loop

This is the perfect go-to knot for tying your hooklength to the end of your fishing mainline.

1 Make a simple loop at the end of the line.

2 Hook the loop over itself.

3 Put your index finger into the large loop and twist it around twice. Then make another half twist.

4 Tuck the small loop into the larger loop.

5 Tighten the knot and a figure of eight will form.

6 Add a little spit before you tighten up.

Further information

Further Help

With the modern-day, accomplished angler, relying heavily on the internet and websites for information, there has never been so much available in terms of fast-track learning for a beginner to the sport. Clubs, tackle shops, fisheries, day and season permit prices and even the weather can be researched prior to your planned fishing trip! We now live in an age where as a beginner, or even the angler who's been a few times and wants to further their knowledge in a particular area of the sport, there's a professional coaching service available.

For any angler in the modern world, the first port of call for information should be The Angling Trust, an organisation that encompasses most areas related to coarse angling, and indeed angling as whole, in the UK. The trust has a dedicated team of experts, coaches, lists of fisheries, tackle shops and all manner of legal advice for individuals and clubs alike. If you prefer the personal approach, then go to your local tackle shop. If they want your trade they should offer sound advice and get you on the road to catching a few fish. A local club is also worth looking at, as there will be seasoned anglers who will have many years of experience behind them and will be glad to help the beginner. Do your research, make sure you have the correct licences and tickets and take time to appreciate all that surrounds you... It's not just about catching fish, it's about the whole journey into a fantastic sport that might just hold you in its grip for life!

Useful websites

www.anglingtrust.net

The Angling Trust, a body that encompasses all manner of fishing from coarse to sea and even game fishing. A host of information on fisheries, tackle shops, angling coaches, legal matters and more.

www.fishinginfo.co.uk

A website dedicated to finding an angling coach, weather apps, tackle shops, methods and even the local weather for when planning your day out.

www.fishing.com

Links to worldwide fishing websites.

www.learntofish.co.uk

A dedicated website to help you find an angling coach and listings of events taking place up and down the country.

www.fish-uk.com

Fisheries, tackle shops and even fishing holidays feature regularly on this website.

Glossary

anal fin a single fin, on the underside of the fish, close to the tail

aquatic larvae larvae that live in the water

bait food used to catch fish

barb a sharp section at the end of a hook that points in the opposite direction of the hook's end; barbs make it harder to extract a hook

barbule a carp's barbules are the slim feelers, located either side of the mouth of the fish

bread flakes pieces of bread, torn from a loaf, used as bait

commercial fishery privately owned waters that are heavily stocked with coarse fish; anglers need to pay to fish here

dead bait dead fish, used as bait

dorsal fin a single fin on the back of a fish

flank the side of an animal's body between the last rib and the hip

gill plate the flap of skin that covers the gills of a fish

glands organs in the body that produce substances such as sweat and tears

legering fishing with the help of ground bait (bait that sinks to the bottom of the river or lake and attracts fish that feed there)

licence official permission; a fishing licence permits the holder to fish in certain waters

non-migratory an animal that stays in its habitat all year round

nymph a young insect

pharyngeal teeth teeth that sit to the back of the mouth, by the throat

predator an animal that hunts and kills other animals for food

prey an animal that is hunted and killed by other animals for food

shoal a large number of fish, swimming together

silt fine sand or clay

specimen an individual animal that is used as an example of its species

specimen fish a fish that is of the typical weight and size of others in the same species

split shot small (often metal) pellets that are used to weigh down fishing line

stillwater a body of water that isn't flowing, such as a lake

territorial an animal that defends its territory (area where it hunts and lives)

toxic poisonous

waggler float a float that is attached by the bottom end only

Index

NATURE DETECTIVE

Become a nature detective and discover how to identify common British wildlife with these fantastic titles:

9780750283410

9781526301574

9781526301185

9780750293211

9780750283427

9780750293235

9780750293259

9780750293273

Let's investigate!

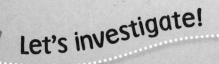